T0375497

Life

Is

BEAUTIFUL

LENFORD THOMPSON

authorHOUSE®

AuthorHouse™
1663 Liberty Drive
Bloomington, IN 47403
www.authorhouse.com
Phone: 1 (800) 839-8640

© 2016 Lenford Thompson. All rights reserved.

No part of this book may be reproduced, stored in a retrieval system, or transmitted by any means without the written permission of the author.

Published by AuthorHouse 03/22/2016

ISBN: 978-1-5049-8545-1 (sc)
ISBN: 978-1-5049-8543-7 (hc)
ISBN: 978-1-5049-8544-4 (e)

Library of Congress Control Number: 2016904478

Print information available on the last page.

Any people depicted in stock imagery provided by Thinkstock are models, and such images are being used for illustrative purposes only. Certain stock imagery © Thinkstock.

This book is printed on acid-free paper.

Because of the dynamic nature of the Internet, any web addresses or links contained in this book may have changed since publication and may no longer be valid. The views expressed in this work are solely those of the author and do not necessarily reflect the views of the publisher, and the publisher hereby disclaims any responsibility for them.

CHAPTER 1

Write a book entitled LIFE IS BEAUTIFUL, which contains your experiences with mental illness and other matters. Your inpatient stays and also your outpatient at the Hospital. In this book write about all the people you have met in these institutions from the man that farts and upsets the staff every time he passes by. Mention how he flicks the lights on and off and how sometimes he does it in the nurses' station and how they hate it! Recall the first time you heard him pass gas and how you uncontrollably burst into laughter and how the Asian lady who was there at the scene of the crime began to snicker as well. I remember saying to her, "I'm not laughing at him I was just not expecting that." She replied, "You should be over here to smell it!" But he was very ill, one of the sickest. I can also recall the day he was to be discharged; they even brought a stretcher because I guess they were not sure if he would be able to make it safely out of the hospital. I'm even laughing as I'm writing this because about four hours later he was once again a patient at the Hospital. The medics took the stretcher with an angry and frustrated Terry right back to 3South, where he once again started farting and messing with the lights.

Mention the Hispanic man Raul, who sometimes when he spoke no one understood. I guess his accent was deeply rooted in his homeland but I remember him clearly saying, as I stood holding the phone having a conversation with my mother, "REMEMBER LIFE IS BEAUTIFUL," which is the basis of this book as it were the inspiration. I remember that one day as he passed by I said, "what's up papi," for that's what I call Hispanic men of whom I am not familiar, he turned around and said "my name no papi its Raul." His name and his words I will never forget, he shook my hands and we became friends. I can also recall one day as we sat in goals group, David, who I will speak of later, was talking a lot that session. The group's director was choosing people to read a paragraph of the pamphlet that was placed in our hands. As each person read it seemed as though David commented on what everyone said, whether it was my turn, Tammy's turn, Raul's and others. Finally Raul got frustrated, he said something in Spanish and then English and as the English words were to be spoken all I heard was, "why you no make nobody else speak you always talk talk talk." In another instance I accidentally walked in on him coming out of the shower butt naked, I said, "sorry papi, I mean sorry Raul," he replied "no worry no worry we boat man." Once again thanks for the words Raul hope to see you on the outside.

How can I forget about my main man Graves, what a very unique name. We met in the outpatient program about five years ago; he was an old fellow who sometimes limps and hunches when he walk and took slow steps.

He shared with me that he had been in and out of mental institutions since he was a child. John was a very great artist I know that for a fact because he has drawn portraits of my family. One thing about John was that he drew pictures of Jesus every day. He draws black Jesus, white Jesus, Jesus with a tan, blue eyed Jesus, brown-eyed Jesus, even green eyed Jesus. John's best friend at the outpatient unit was a Mexican American woman name Roxy, what's funny about Roxy is that she refers to herself in the third person. For example instead of saying, "I love you," she says "Roxy loves you. Well Roxy, I love you and Graves.

Now I'm going to speak about another one who I call my main man; Rocky. He worked in the inpatient unit and always looked out for me. We had an on again off again relationship. I met him at the inpatient unit and instantly knew he was a cool dude. In September of 2014, after being out of the unit for 4 years I was once again back in 3South. When I saw him again he looked disappointed to see me, because I know that the last thing he wanted was to see me back in the hospital. Whenever he was off I would ask, "When is Rocky working." He always looked out for me. In that same stay I became very ill, the sickest I had ever been. My behavior became sporadic and I was often placed in a place called "the quiet room." In there were only four walls and a mattress on the ground. I despised and resented the quiet room but I came to understand the purpose for its existence. At nights he watched over me and made sure I was doing all right. Like Samson, he had dreads and maybe that's where he got his strength from, because I have seen him throw many men into that room. I love him like a brother and friend.

Now lets get to the aforementioned David, the reason for Raul's frustration. David was a nice guy, but some of the staff and patients thought he talked incessantly. He was a very intelligent guy who always had an opinion, which seemed to stem from his frustration with his position in life. He was adopted and I think that played a major role with his frustrations. We shared a room, an idea in which neither of us were quite fond of, but managed to compromise. During group, a time for us to share, he often contributed and gave these riddles that no one understood. The group's leader would act as though he/she understood, but they would be just as confused as the rest of us. I wish well for David, I hope he will find comfort that he missed from his parents and has longed forever since. On the day he was discharged we hugged and said farewell. That's the thing about farewells at 3South we often send each other away with good wishes hoping that this parting would be for an extended period of time, but knowing that one day we would again see each other.

When I came back to Three South the first person to greet me was a guy named Jonathan. At first I was nervous being the new guy, but you can see good in a person before you even shake their hands and I saw that in Jonathan. Jonathan was a very funny guy, he had this thing called the one word song. The verses and chorus were one word. One day I said "John sing Love" I hear him respond "Loooovvvveeeee" and that's it his entire song in one word.

We eventually became roommates along with another patient Michael. Me, big Mike and Jonathan were like the three amigos. Mike was a little on the heavy side, Jonathan was in shape and I had a big gut. So every morning we would encourage each other to do push-ups but of course Jonathan did more than all of us. In the mornings we would have these sessions called 'share your dream.' We would go one after another sharing what we dreamt the night before. Jonathan had a dream he was in a wrestling ring fighting with John Cena; I cannot recall whom he said won the match, but I would put all my chips on Cena. Then Mike would share his dreams; however I cannot recall what his dreams were about. I myself suffered with insomnia, a condition that was partly responsible for me ending up in Three South. Since it was difficult for me to sleep I had no dreams to tell. Nevertheless, one day my rest will be sweet and I'll have a myriad of dreams to share with big Mike and John. Eventually Big Mike and John moved on. and oh how I missed them both, but I have their memories in my heart. I hope to see them once again and share a laugh and tell of our dreams.

On the first day back I entered the TV room, a place where all the patients come, I took a seat near a Hispanic man, he was eating skittles while fully engaged in the program on the television. He offered me some of the candy but I politely declined. This man whom I had never met and whose name I was not able to learn turned to me and said, "you look like you've been through a lot." If I was in solitary state I would've shed tears, for his words were so true. I started taking medication when I was about seventeen years old, but the medications were only for depression. Now looking back at my desperate troubled life I wish depression was the only reason I am subjected to these pills with their many side effects and their addictive nature. Some hate them, but have come to realize that they might not be able to function or live without them. As for me I am also, as of now, unable to live a normal life without my medication. As I mentioned before I suffer from insomnia so something as basic as sleeping I am not able to do without the use of medication. I remember I once picked up a book that was collecting dust on my shelf, the basis of this book was how to naturally overcome mental illness, I read about two chapters and then decided to discard all my medication into the toilet (what was I thinking). About two days later I had to run to the psychiatrists to refill the pills. The psychiatrists seem to think that this is a fact, which has been written in concrete that I will not maintain a life without my medication, but I know for a fact that nothing lasts forever. I will recover from this disease and my colleagues will also.

I remember this lady Catherine, we traveled in the same vehicle to get to our outpatient programs. The van would drop Catherine off at St. Vincent and me at

At the Hospital. I had not seen Catherine for a while and when I glimpsed I could see the pain in her face. I was not sure if it was her at first, because she looked gloomy, sad and desperate. It seemed something had changed inside of her. I went up and greeted her and immediately she recognized me; her arms opened and we shared a warm embrace. I remember in one instance she was writing something in a book, she informed me that it was a poem. Being such a fan of poetry I inquired if I could see what she was working on and she replied, "of course when I'm finished." I patiently waited because I also write poetry and I enjoyed reading other's work. She finally finished but before she allowed me to partake of the poem she picked up the phone and seemed very content with the person she was speaking to on the phone. I patiently waited some more for the conclusion of the conversation. I was not paying attention to her conversation but I could hear words such as love and baby. When she finally came off the phone she read me the words of the poem, beautiful words from a beautiful lady.

Now lets get to Segundo, I'm not sure of his ethnicity, but I am aware of his timid ways and his routines. He would pace up and down the hallway all day, only taking a break for mealtime or group. He would stare at the clock every time he passed by. I would often greet him with a hi or a nod of the head. Segundo was my weatherman, after about two weeks I stopped watching television and because of that I never saw the news so I would not know the weather. So one day he came near to me and said, "its gonna rain today," and sure enough it rained. I hope he gets a job at NBC 4 as a meteorologist.

I love these people. Many live in their past for their future seems quite bleak, but man they can make me laugh. I remember this one guy, he picked up the phone, and he didn't dial any number but started speaking as though someone was on the other end. I could understand his reasoning though, being inpatient makes them yearn to hear a familiar voice even if it's their own. They miss home and the way they use to be, happy children who are now sad men, who wish things were better. I am more privileged than most of them, but I understand their struggles, to be attacked by an invisible foe such as depression, schizophrenia and all these other names. Some of us because of illegal drugs now take psychiatric ones, they both have side effects but one wonders which one is more beneficial, which one will get you closer to God.

CHAPTER 2
Sutton Park

Having a mental illness is not the end of the road, although it has somewhat detoured me from getting steady work. I have had many jobs, from working in an arcade as a ride attendant at New Roc City, delivering wholesale food, Park Nursing and Rehabilitation, and at Playland Amusement Park.

At Playland I made dog tags similar to those worn by our military service men and women. I was not properly trained for this task, but I learned through trial and error. I remember making a dog tag for Donavan Pink who attended my church and was like me, a victim of this disease. The tag included his name and address for he would sometimes wonder off. Donavan also suffered from seizures so his concerned mother requested that I make him a dog tag in case of emergencies. He would often have seizures during our church services, the service would come to an abrupt halt as his mother and sister attended to his needs. I believe that one day Donavan will recover from his illness and I know that this will also be true for me as well.

I was a housekeeper better known as a janitor at Park Nursing and Rehabilitation. Although I did not particularly love the job I appreciated it. Having a job meant that I did not have to borrow money from my parents for a haircut and things of that nature. Nonetheless the thing I looked forward to and enjoyed the most were the patients. They were like grown children. There's a saying that goes "once a man twice a child" which was evident working within a nursing home. I loved working with my coworkers, but I had a special Campbell Tomato Soup love for those patients.

Mention the lady at Sutton Park who prayed for me while I was coming off my lunch break. I had just finished eating, I cannot remember the meal but I can remember her kind words. My coworkers Garth, Errol and I were walking when this old gray-headed lady who was confined to her wheelchair approached us. She signaled with her finger that I should come to her and I obeyed. She then requested that I hold her hand I once again obeyed and that's when I'll never forget the day that sweet old lady prayed for me and I believe one day that prayer will come to fruition.

How can I forget Lena Hamm, who I call Lena ham and cheese. Lena was a sweet old lady who always kissed me on the cheek. The nurses warned me that I should not greet her in this manner and I yielded to their request. One day I came over to the seat that she sat everyday next to her bestie. Just as she always does she reached for my cheek but I declined. I could see in her aged yet beautiful face that she was hurt by my response, she turned her head and said, "I'm not talking to you anymore." Twenty minutes later she forgot the whole thing she smiled at me as I was mopping the floor longing for my lunch break. I will never forget you my Lena Hamm and Cheese.

At Sutton Park it seemed as though everyone smoked from the staff to the patients. There was this particular man named Mr. Sutton, we often joked that it was his nursing home. I came over to him one day and said, "Mr. Sutton when you gonna quit smoking cigarettes?" he quickly replied, "When they stop making them. I smirked because I had not expected such a clever response to my question. I do not know if this clever old man has passed or if he is still at Sutton Park smoking those cigarettes but I hope neither is true.

I also remember this sweet old lady who suffered from Alzheimer's. She would frequently ask the patients and the staff, "Where am I?" and everyday I just smiled and wished she could remember. One day I thought I would help her out and tell her of her location. On this particular day I sat waiting for Ms. Jones to ask that all so popular question, of which I believed deserved a response. Ms. Jones true to form said, "Where am I ?" I put down my mop approached her and replied, "you're in America Ms. Jones. She sharply replied, "I know that ya jackass!" I could not help but burst into a silent fit of laughter, I wonder if she would remember this, but probably not. She was the only person that I can recall to ever give me such an answer like that and it not upset me. I think of her response all the time, which I share with my family, and we all laugh out loud.

I remember the first time I was admitted into the psychiatric hospital in 2007. I was at the Hospital, I had many visitors but the support that I appreciate the most was my fellow workers from Sutton Park. We sat and had many conversations, but never mentioned work. The funny thing is having bad memory, a side effect of some of my medications, I cannot remember all their names, but I can remember the support. I know they longed for me to, as they say, get into my right mind, I tried but it was not an easy task. At night in the hospital, due to my insomnia, I would pace back and forth in a room with two other patients. They would be fast asleep and I would be jealous because of the fact that the most sleep I would get was about two hours. But the one thing I thought about the one thing I longed for as I would pace the room was my visits. Thanks for the support.

CHAPTER 3
Ladies

Women have always played a significant role in my life from my mother to my aunties, who I will speak of later because I have so many. Right now let's speak of Tammy, the Hispanic lady who speaks frequently of her son who had passed. She walks around with a Walkman most days she speaks to herself while crying. Some may think she is crazy, but I believe that those tears were shed for her beloved who is no more. I remember that we were in a group one day and she gave an analogy of a baby who cannot stand for of course it is a babe who has yet to learn to walk. She illustrated vividly how this child searches for things to hold on to that can hold their weight. The baby grasps for the couch, the table and several other objects, but we who are grown and of full age are still in search of things to bare our weight. When she spoke those powerful words I uncontrollably clapped and said "true words." Although I am not a parent who has experienced the loss of a child I feel her pain. Keep your head up Tammy, someday you will reunite with your son and will listen to those songs together.

Let's talk about my good friend Kareema nice lady who tells me every time I eat in the morning, "Finish your breakfast." Some might think she is uneducated because of her appearance, but she's much more than that. I remember her handing me a tissue while I hung my head and asking "why are you crying?" Such a simple act of kindness mean the most to me. That's how Kareema was, always showing small acts of kindness. One of the side effects of my medication is that I often salivate from the mouth without noticing, Kareema would always silently signal to me and I would know to take my towel off my shoulder and dry my mouth and sometimes even my tears. Its funny when you judge a book before reading the last page, you never get to experience the best parts. I hope I meet her again one day and hand her a tissue for a change when life gets tough.

The girl who handed me the bible; She was very cute, petite and humble. She handed me the bible, I took a quick look and then handed it back. She said that the bible was dedicated to Jehovah (I wished she would give it back to me). Anyway she took it back and handed me an old tattered one with a crumbled cover, missing pages and the ones that were there were torn. I believe this situation humbled me to know that even if a bible is battered they still have the same words and the same message. She was only at the inpatient program for a day and the sad thing about all of this is that I didn't read that bible much, maybe because of the fact that I was in despair, I wouldn't even pray with words, my tears were my prayer.

After I left the inpatient department, I took all my possessions home, but I misplaced that old but valuable book, so as I write this right now, I see the white bag which held my possessions I thought maybe the bible was somewhere in that bag which the hospital provided and sure enough I found the bible with its crumbled cover, missing words and highlighted pages. I wish her well and I hope if she has an extra bible she could present it to someone else and I hope the recipient might read it, appreciate it, and buy a highlighter.

While in Three South I reunited with two of my friends from the outpatient program Laurie and Laura, I would like to first mention Laurie. Being bipolar she would have her mood swings which I had myself so I understood her episodes. She had red hair and beautiful eyes. One thing I know about Laurie is if it seems like she is not in a good mood, don't bother her, but that's a part of being human, you never know what side of the bed you're going to wake up on. One day as she passed she gave me advice just by simply saying, "Keep your chin up." I see the best in Laurie in her ups and even in her downs. I hope she also keeps her chin up.

I met another lady at Three South, her name was Monique, nice lady but it seems that someone or something was holding her back from her true purpose in life. Her pastor, who she was always grateful to see, comforted her. The day that she was to be discharged she handed me a track. A track is a pamphlet, which usually contains words of comfort from the bible. These are the words she wrote within the track.: "*Dear Lenford things will get better, trust God always, he's never late always on time and he knows and understands your pain and suffering. Read the book of Psalms by king David and Proverbs for wisdom. May God continue to have you in his care, I love you*"- Monique. Thank you Monique and I pray you find your true purpose in life.

There was a lady at the day program, a Jewish lady; her name was Maytal, morning dew. She was my best friend, one of the most humble people you will ever meet. Because of her attributes I plan on making her legacy go on by naming my first daughter Maytal. We would walk to lunch together, so since we did that everyone assumed we were in a relationship, but I love her too much to ever destroy our friendship. She was also admitted with me the last time I stayed at Three South, but that time she seemed different, like someone had taken something from her that had much value, something precious. I loved speaking to her, but this time she slept all day and those rare instances when she would step out of her room I would rush over to her just to talk and reminisce. However those chats were always short, she would always say, "Later Lenford" and head back into her room. I prayed that she would get better. My beautiful sister, wonderful lady, gracious heart, beautiful soul, you are and will always be my morning dew.

Sister Dear

Cry your tears sister dear
Cause ain't nobody gonna cry them for you
But call on me when
Your eyes require tissue
Foggy is the morning
But others have made it through
The night is that way too
But your joy will come
Though many days of sorrow
Are gone and done
Face your fears Sister Dear
For your fears have confronted you
Laugh and smile Sister Child
For it'll all be worth it
In a while.

CHAPTER 4
Ten West

In church I refer to the older men as uncle the older women as auntie, elderly women as grandma and those close to my age as sister and brother. I guess you can say I have a big family.

What can I say about church and my spirituality? I was practically born there, while in my mother's womb I was a member of The Church of God Seventh Day. I sang in the choir and collected the tithes and offering. I tried my best to respect their rules and adopted their precepts. I would pray for the forgiveness of my sins and those of my family and friends and peace on earth, but at the same time the only time I knelt was when times were better.

When I first got ill with this condition, that I despise so much, I used to confide in my mother for I appreciated her input, but she not being aware of the severity of my illness, suggested that I should pray about it. Being a woman of faith, which is also her name, and seeming unable to bare this believed if I prayed God would deliver me. So at her request I prayed about it, but the depression still lingered and those were dark days. Still, my church family who I will talk more about, they have always supported me. Church has always been my anchor, my backbone. I cannot imagine my life without them especially my church in America, 10 West Third Street has been my home since 1994.

I remember how much Uncle Brown would recite the same prayer to collect the tithes and offering. How every time you would ask him a question I mean any question he would give you a one-word reply.

I can recall how Pastor Seixas would smile from ear to ear the entire service. How he would always try to guess what word the preacher would say next.

My Bishop, Bishop McCallum met him in 1994. Since I have been in the church many people have left the congregation and you can see that it has affected him very much. My family has been one of the few that have remained. Nonetheless, gradually more came to replace those who have left the congregation. Now he smiles. One famous thing about Bishop was his tendency to play people off with his organ. If someone has been on the mic too long, he would play a tune on the organ, which he sat on all service. When there was a baby dedication Bishop Mac would not be able to pronounce the baby's name, he would even add or subtract a letter. When he sang songs directly from the songbook he would sing the wrong words. Go on playing your organ.

The lunchroom is in the basement so some of the church sisters would have a hard time going down the stairs. I would take their lunch bags and guide them and after lunch I would bring them back up again. One such lady is my auntie Givens. Auntie Givens is such a particular lady. I remember she would park next to the parking meter every Sabbath and since there was not free parking on Saturday she would give me quarters to place in the meter so that she would not get a ticket. I mean service was all day from 9am-6pm. that's a lot of quarters. Auntie Givens knows I love sweet potatoes so she always made sure she gave me some. Love you auntie.

I remember how auntie Ety much like Lena Hamm would give me kisses on my cheek. She always asked me when I would get married and I always answered "soon." She was constantly in pain, but you wouldn't know that based on her demeanor. She always seemed vibrant, but rarely stayed the whole day I guess it was due to the pain she was experiencing. I would escort her to uncle Brown's car, open the door and tell her I'll see her next week. One day she'll be able to meet my wife and kids.

How can I forget Auntie Sharon, I love this lady, very hilarious person wherever she was she could go into funny mode. She could make people laugh at a funeral. The thing about auntie Sharon is she loves to sing. She knew a quarter of the song, the rest she would make up, there were even times she inserted her own name into the songs, for the example, "Sharon loves you Lord." When we go downstairs to the lunchroom that's when the jokes start flying. Auntie Sharon would have everyone in stitches. In rare conditions we would go back and forth, going into battle I always knew auntie Sharon would win, but I always try my luck. Maybe next time.

Lets get to my auntie Richie, very calm and would never really show too many emotions, but man when the Holy Ghost got a hold of her she seemed different, almost angelic. When you hear auntie testify it sounds like tears mixed with pain and you cant help but be in awe. Her and my mother are best friends and that made us closer. I love her as if she were my own mother.

My big brother Dwight, who is also my best friend, is about five years older than me. Our friendship did not start the first time we saw each other. Now the teenagers, including Dwight, did not really talk to us much. Eventually all of Dwight's friends left the church, leaving Dwight behind and that's how we became friends. There's not a friend like my big brother. If we go to a restaurant he always wants the check no matter how much you volunteer. It goes even further than that, his moral support and compassion are unmatched. I remember we went to a wedding reception there was a lot of alcohol. Being on medication I knew that I was not a good idea to drink, but due to the occasion I decided to have two cups. Dwight quickly reminded me that I should not be drinking and I put it down. I would take this whole book to tell of everything Dwight has done for me. At one point I was not working so he gave me money without me asking. He decided to make me the Godfather to his son Jayden, but much like my job at Play Land I was not properly trained on how to do this task. I rarely bought him presents like other Godparents. Jayden used to cry a lot so I got someone to make him a shirt that said, "When I cry people seem to pay attention to me." I love Dwight's wife, my big sister Carleen. She is the catalyst in me writing songs. I only knew how to write poetry so the transition was hard at first, but after a while I got it. I have been writing music ever since.

My little sister Roshelle Brown, which we all refer to by her pet name, Shannet, sang most of the songs

I wrote, Beautiful dark skin girl from Brooklyn. Her voice seemed to fit every song. There is one particular song that I wrote called "New Jerusalem," which speaks of life on the New Earth. Whenever she sings that song those who hear it seem deeply affected, not only by the sound but the powerful message behind it. I have many other songs but she sings this one the most. Thanks Net Net for singing with your soul what I have written with my pen.

That brings me to my little brother Lyshon. A Jamaican dude that grew up in Guyana, at first we could not understand his accent, but we both understood friendship. We have never had a fight or argued and I would love for that to stay the same. Lyshon can be very mischievous. I remember when we had a church convention at a hotel in Connecticut. One day the fire alarm went off and guess who was the culprit. He has done many other things, but like a good big brother I tried to counsel him and give him advice. Heard he's stepping up in church and contribute more in the services, it's a great thing when young men, especially black men, give their lives to God. Do your thing bro. I have been baptized fifteen years and God has always stayed the same. Love you little brother I wish you well-both hands on the wheel.

Lyshon has two other siblings, Lindell and Fiona. Fiona caught my eyes as soon as I saw her. A beautiful half Black half Indian woman. I remember one Sabbath I preached a message. When the message ends the custom was everyone either shake the messengers hand or share a hug seeing her in line to greet me I became very nervous but also excited, finally it was her turn, I saw her hands not knowing if I was going to be blessed with a hug and not a shake, it turned out to be a hand shake. But I knew eventually it will be more than a handshake.

At one point while dating Fiona I decided to rededicate my life to God, so our conversations wouldn't involve words that was inappropriate, and seeing that she wasn't a devoted Christian we would read the bible and pray over the phone. Eventually we broke up, I backslid but stayed in church and our bond was broken, but when she visits we speak. I will never forget my princess Fiona hope she would find her prince.

My little brother Darius what can I say about this guy, I see a lot of me in him, and my sister seems to concur. In church I would often recite poetry and short readings. Not knowing that my little brother was listening, one Sabbath morning he was on the program, he stood up and took the mic, he read a poem that blew me away, I think when the poem was over I clapped the loudest. I have witnessed him get baptized and grow when it comes to God. Dar (as we sometimes call him) had a temper not like the one Jesus had in his temple, but I think that because of the level of respect we had for each other we've never clashed. As I write these words, I am struggling with things and circumstances, which seem too much for me to bare. He has recently got baptized, and what I should've told is that he will have great times, everything is going fine, the household is happy, but those bad times are lurking, but you are marked to do great things so Dar, Darius, Dizzy, little brother like how Laurie said to me I say to you: Keep your chin up.

Ejohn was the only person in the crew who liked baseball, the rest of us were basketball junkies. I thank him for bringing me to my first sporting event out of the four major sports, it was cold but I appreciated the experience. We called Ejohn the human GPS. He literally knows most of the city and other places. If you are lost call my big brother and he will direct you to your destination. For a long time everyone wondered what the E in EJohn meant but he refused to disclose that information, until one day he gave in, but I will never tell. Ejohn is a cool dude, he used to stammer but no one made fun of him. We're family and family should build each other up than to tear them down. Ejohn has done so much for me, he got me a job at Victory Food Service. This was the hardest job I had ever had but good looking out big brother, I appreciate it.

Now lets get to my light skin brother from a different mother, Devane. The funny thing is that it use to be that when we would play basketball, Devane used to be the student and I would be the master. He was a good student, but now my little brother has become the master and always shows me things I did not show him. Devane's nickname is bread, his little brother calls him that the most. I don't know how that came to be. I say its because he was so light skin like a loaf of bread. We were both a part of a Basketball team in a church league; Jermaine (coach) Junior (assistant coach) the players were; myself, Darius, Devane, EJohn, Lyshon, Dwight, and Dane. When my brother Devane gets into basketball mode watch out! He's yelling at the other teammates, he seems frustrated and fed up, but the funny thing about it is when the game is over he's the nicest person in the world. His brother decided to get baptized, I would love if he would follow his brother's lead. Little brother I love you and want the best for you. Remember God is the answer even when they've changed the questions.

CHAPTER 5
Sis One & Sis Two

Now let's speak of my princess, my youngest sister Malika. When she was born she did not have much hair so I call her baldy, I remember when she started to grow a full head of hair I called her baldy and she replied, "I'm not bald no more call me hairy." Malika and I are thirteen years apart, but we're like twins. I remember that I sometimes have to take care of her in the summer. When we went out her hair would be a mess, so I put a hat on it since I could not braid and her clothes were mix match. Looking back at it I smile. People must of thought I was her father who cant take care of his daughter.

We, mostly me, used to order Malika around; "Malika turn on the TV, turn it off, get me something to drink, get me something to eat." One day she got fed up and exclaimed, "Don't you have two hands?" That's when I knew my reign was over. I'm not sure if she knows how much I love her, although I tell her time and time again. She and I share a bond, considering that we both almost died on several occasions, but those are stories for another book. I can truly say that when she hurts so do I. When she's sick I wish I could take her place. Malika is very involved in church, she sings, prays, and does praise dance, she reads and one time she even preached. She and my father would always be the last ones to leave church and amongst the first to come the next week.

Malika's relationship with my parents was different from Kamoy's and mine. My father spent more time with her being that she was born in America. She knew him her entire childhood, while Kamoy and I hardly saw our father. My sister Kamoy actually thought our Uncle Horace was her father. We only spent two years apart from our mother so our memories of her were fresh in our thoughts. I wrote something on Facebook when it was Malika's birthday and at the end of the writing I wrote I loved her like a fat kid loves cake. I sometimes call her Malika, Molly, Hairy, but she will always be my baldy.

Now this book would not be complete unless I speak of my other sister, the middle child, Kamoy. We grew up like twins, went everywhere together did everything together which including getting our many butt whoopings. I can't even count the amount of hits we accumulated over the years. Living in an apartment building we did not have many friends on the block and we did not go outside so we had to make our own games to entertain ourselves. We had one game where we crushed a piece of paper in a ball and hit it with composition notebooks. The object of the game was to keep the crumbled paper up as long as possible and the one to make it fall would lose. Growing up we did not have much, I remember me and Kamoy went to a friend's house and played Monopoly. We loved the game, but thought our parents could not afford it so from memory I recreated it using cardboard. That actually encouraged me to later invent my own game called Double UP. There were certain things we were not allowed to do like celebrate Halloween so we could not go trick or treating. One year my mom allowed us to go trick or treating, we did not have much so we had no costumes so we had to wear regular clothes, I guess that's why we did not get much candy. I will never forget that.

I remember when Kamoy went to college, me and my father dropped her off at the bus station. While in the car we joked and enjoyed each other's company like the good old days. When she got to the bus station I waited for the bus with her. While on line I tried holding in the tears but I could not, we hugged, I cried, she left. We had to face the reality that we may not see each other as often as we would've liked. In my family we don't say "I love you" so I didn't get an opportunity to say that to Kamoy when the bus came and my best friend left. After some years she came home for good and I was glad because I got my twin back. I love this girl.

It's funny because I always wanted a brother, but I would never trade my sisters for anything in the world.

CHAPTER 6
Welcome to America

I remember happier days when I was a child, knowing not what depression was, having never heard the word schizophrenia. My job was to be a child and those were wonderful times. I was born on the island of Jamaica and this following reading sums it all up. Its entitled BED BUGS.

BED BUGS

Drink forget about your sorrows for a while try to remember when you were a child, life was better then, we were poor but we were all we had. I remember that my mother, my father, my sister and I, all slept in one bed back when we lived in Jamaica. My father was usually overseas, he worked in the U.S trying to make a better life for us, but when he came home once again we all slept in one bed, my mother and father were at the top, their feet laid next to our faces and at times became our pillows. But once again daddy went back to the U.S and now there were three. Soon after it was just little sister and I because mommy joined daddy where she cried for us daily. While she cried we laughed with our new mother Auntie Winsome, uncle Horace became our father. Our five cousins now became our brothers and sisters, but after two years we said goodbye to them too, now auntie cried for us. Reunited and it felt so good with mommy and daddy in a strange land where we all slept in different beds, soon after different rooms, we once dreamt the same dream we once dreamt of each other, I wonder if our nightmares are the same. Sister in college now so now I sleep in her bed, for mine had too many demons. Maybe I could dream her dreams, see if they're the same as mine, see what makes her cry, see what makes her smile. They say some drink to remember and some drink to forget well I wish that I forget these present days and remember a time when we all slept in one bed.

Making the transition from the Jamaican school system to the American was not so smooth for me. One thing that would scar me for a while was the American children taunting me and my sister because of the way we dressed and our accents. I found it strange that in public schools in America no one wore uniforms, I was shocked to know that this was the reality. We wore one pair of sneakers for most of the school year and our clothes were not the best. We LIVED in Payless and thought we were somehow like the other kids, but we were still taunted knowing that our clothes and shoes were cheap. We just wanted to fit in with everyone. I remember buying fake Timberland boots from Payless everyone gave me sarcastic comments, but I wasn't an idiot; I knew enough to know what was going on. What made my days in school even worse was the fact that I was illiterate so half of the school day I would be in my regular class and the other half was spent in a special education classroom. It was embarrassing, the children were younger than me, but it was beneficial because I learned how to read. I even won the spelling bee and had a B average.

Skip to High School. I would be labeled a bum, meaning that I didn't have the best haircut and couldn't afford not even one foot of the latest sneaker. My clothes seemed as though they were handed down. I reluctantly accepted the bum status, which included free lunch. Now the counterpart of a bum is a pretty boy. The pretty boy wore five different pairs of sneakers for the school week. They almost never ate school lunch, they would order Chinese food and they had all the girls. I was a bum until I got a job. The summer before my junior year I stacked up. Instead of buying clothes to go to work I wore the uniform, instead of buying a big lunch I got some quarters and ate from the vending machine, got me a snicker and a bag of chips and drank water. I saved a couple thousands. So when it was time to enter into my junior year I moved up in the ranks from bum to pretty boy, but I still ate the school lunches. As shy as I was I started to attract females, I had the best clothes, best sneakers, now I felt like I now could fit in, cause that's all I ever wanted. In my mind I started criticizing people on how they dressed, not realizing that I had become those kids from elementary and middle school who taunted me. I was so disappointed in myself. I still dress well, not to show off, but to have a defense mechanism because of what I went through in school. But to all the mothers who can't afford to send your kids to school in the latest clothes, who live in Payless and your kids wear hand me downs I can relate. To the mother who has to work three to four jobs hoping that their son could make it to the NBA, keep your head up. If you're fresh off the boat or if you were born here, remember better must come.

The first apartment we lived in was in a basement. I remember the kids that lived on the first floor would run up and down and play and scream and we could hear it clearly so my father would take a broom and bang on the ceiling. We eventually all became friends, the kids were Mikhail and Kadeem and their parents were Stanley and Leila who we affectionately called Lamby and Ricey. Since we had not been in the country that long I was trying to get acclimated to the system. One day Stanley and Leila took us to McDonalds. They went to the counter and ordered a family meal so I was disappointed, because I thought we all had to be a family in order to eat the meal. Wow I've come a long way. This reading is dedicated to Stanley and Leila I was supposed to read it at the renewing of their vows, but ended up in the hospital so I hope they're reading it now.

Lamby and Ricey

This is dedicated to Stanley and Leila, whose names I always thought were Lamby and Ricey. I was always familiar with the name Ricey, because my dad's also shared the same nickname, but when I heard Lamby I was like "what? Who would name their child Lamby?" Some call him Stanley, but to me its still Lamby. I see that their love is special and holy. I use the word holy, because Lamby and Ricey are people of faith.

When I came here from Jamaica, my sister and I lived in a private house, we were in the basement and Ricey, Lamby, and their children Mikhail and Kadeem lived on the first floor. Its funny because when we lived in Jamaica my mother would send us beautiful pictures of life in America so coming here I thought there would be money trees, but when I got here I found a different reality. Nonetheless Lamby and Ricey made our time in America lovely. They did as they say "showed us the ropes," we rode in the subway for the first time with them, they were the first ones to bring my sister, Kamoy, and I to the movies. I do not remember the film but I do recall the experience, it was memorable.

You know there's some people who come into your life and you feel blessed that they did. Ricey used to come downstairs when my parents were not around and check on us and make sure that we were okay and I love you for that Ricey. If you notice I'm elaborating on my experience with these beautiful souls, because that's all I know. I don't know what they did or helped you with, I don't know your story, but if they touched your life then I'm sure you are also blessed.

I appreciate there love like the love God has for us. I often refer to myself as a church boy, but now that I am grown I guess I should start referring to myself as a churchman. I can recall that Ricey and Lamby would invite us to church and finally me and my sister went and their son Kadeem preached a very inspiring message and I was blessed. They also supported me when I preached my message at my church, they even *recorded it and now I have that memory to watch time and time again.*

Ricey and Lamby were blessed with four sons. Every time Ricey got pregnant we would swear she was going to have a daughter so that Lamby would finally have his little girl, but they never did. However, we always felt like they had daughters anyway, because they took Kamoy and Malika as their own. There are so many more stories that I can tell about these two beautiful and kind people but I would never have enough time. The love that a man has for a woman is special, the Bible states that a man should leave his parents and cleave to his wife, and even now he's still holding on. Lamby never let go.

CONCLUSION

Life sometimes doesn't seem fair. Some take vows of silence, because the times that we did speak no one listened. That's all we mentally ill folks require, someone to listen. Listen to the times when tears flowed like a river more numerous than the sand. When they say Happy Birthday, but your breath could not muster up the strength to blow out the light on top of the candle so you call on your tears to do the job. At first it was just depression, but now its much more, sometimes it feels like us crazy people are the most sane for we've been through insanity, but better must come. I always use this phrase that some of us hurt more than a hospital, and this statement is so true, our wounds aren't visible so they get less attention. "There's nothing wrong they say snap out of it, but when it rains it pours.

I couldn't include everyone I know or have seen in this book, but if you will read this book it would be as if we've already met. Throughout all your mess ups and mishaps, the times you feel like giving up, when everyone has given up on you take the advice that my good friend Raul gave me: REMEMBER LIFE IS BEATIFUL.

Below is a series of poems I have written throughout the years. These poems are near and dear to my heart and represent people and time and personal experiences. I hope you find one that represents you.

MY CITY

I shed tears for my city
At rains at every funeral
That means God is crying with me
These four square miles are filled with violence

But if God can make the suicidal put the gun
Then he can make you his children
shine brighter than the sun
So with evil be not overcome
Dem belly full
While my people are starving
So eat this food for thought
And let me know how taste.

WHITE T

I'm tired of seeing shirts with R.I.P on em
Candles on a corner with a light on em
Lord out here is very dark shine light on em
Get roses by the picture but they can't smell em.

WHEN NIGHT FALLS

When night falls
The clouds most visible are the ones
Which surrounds the moon and
is lit by its beautiful light
Its light makes your face alone glows
And that glow attracts my mind, body and soul
Now like the clouds I surround my moon

When night falls
Then the sun rises
Like the moon you disappear
And like the clouds
I remain here waiting for the night.

BREAD POF SORROW

God is fair
But it feels as if life isn't
Some people have money for breakfast
While others eat sleep for dinner
Empty stomach
Empty bowl
Empty pocket
Empty bowl
Now like a baptized sinner
Were on the brink of death
Yet a prayer away from life
We choose the first
Forsake the latter
For we'd rather
Embrace the unknown
Discarding milk and honey
To partake and in indulge in the bread of sorrow
Prospering today

Only to perish tomorrow
To the untrained eyes we are
straighter than the arrow
While in actuality our path is as crooked as the bow

ISLAND TEARS

If it wasn't for the stars if
If it was for the moon
Jamaica would me on total darkness
Help is not coming any time soon
The youths plates are empty
So they throw away there spoons
And take up stronger steel that take life
If you live by the sword you might
die by a knife in your back
Mama begged son please come out of the cold
But we don't listen we turn back
The street lights are on
Flash lights turn on
They say that life goes on
But what a cruel world for a baby to born
Pot ole mash up dem foot bak
THEY are so cold
You could only trust a politician
To cause more division

THEY tell us what THEY think we should be told
Mold us to a point that THEY can
hold our live in THEIR hands
Whether country or town
They only show up when election time comes around
Is it a crime to be black
The oppressors left J.A a long time a go
So why is it black on black crime?

COFFEE

I sat to have coffee with two dead
men while I was still living
Malcolm who at to my left
And martin sitting on my right
Malcolm stirred the coffee
Martin added milk
I added brown and white sugar
Martin stirred
I got some questions I said
Questions for the dead
Martin are you really free at last
Was unity worth THEIR gun blast
Malcolm were all your means really necessary
Of course my brother he says

So why were your so called brothers
part of the reason you're dead

Martin was it worth turning both cheeks
Martin has a holiday Malcolm
don't you deserve one too
Of course my brotha' I do
Martin you should have seen me
use my boss' bathroom
It didn't say black or white
Some even say men or women
Malcolm you missed the beatings
of Amadu and Rodney king
I know you would've started a rally
Martin you would've sung let freedom ring.
Martin and Malcolm all is not well though
we are the minority we are the
majority within the jail cells.
Our brothas and sistas
Call each other niggas
They sing about murder and guns
While I read of the end
In Revelation chater1
Well I guess my dreaming is coming to its end
So I bid you good day Mr. X and Mr. King
I enjoyed our chat and the coffee

Maybe next time we invite Marcus Garvey.

MIRROR

Mirror mirror on the wall
I wish you would lose the grip of that nail
And to the floor plunge and fall
You say I'm too fat
You say I'm too short
You say my lips are too big
And my skin is too dark
You stupid mirror I really hate you
Telling me my eyes are too brown
That they should be blue

Mirror mirror you can stay
For today me and my mama had a chat
She said child you are not too short
And you are not too fat
You look just fine in the skin you were born in
Your lips are the right size
And they go perfectly
With those pretty brown eyes

CHURCH SHOES

Don't be mad mama,
But there's something I must tell you
don't cry don't be sad mama
Although I did what you had bid me not to do
I messed up and got dirt on my church shoes
How'd it happened you say
Well the only way
By traveling wide dirt roads that have been paved
I forbade the straight and narrow that Jesus gave
and kept on walking in dirty shame
Down there on Devil's Lane
Then pretty soon the rains came
The dirt was changed to mud
As my tears became as blood
But through it mama from dusk till dawn
I always kept my church shoes on

BEAUTY

They say that beauty lies in the eyes of the beholder
Well they told the truth
For this night these eyes behold only you
Beautiful lady
She keeps smiling even when times get shady
With the strength of a man not only in the physical

Mother of my child

The pride of her father

My significant other

With her standing by my side why

would I care about the fall

Miss light skin

Miss dark skin

Miss short

Miss tall

Brown skin sista

My queen of Sheba

I am her Solomon

Her king

Royalty

Cant sing

So I write her poetry

Can't give her the world

Only because it's not big enough

My lady's not a fool

Stern woman of God

Who loves him first then quenches my thirst

Hugs me cause I can't hug myself

Kisses my lips even after we've said I do love you

But love we more

Her love has opened my door

Now only God can close it

Love her more than mamas cooking
Don't care who knows it
Flesh of my flesh
Bone of my bone
Honey I'm home
But this house could never be a home
If she's not within the walls
My heart is not a heart
If the beats don't repeat her name
Beauty, beauty, beauty
If she leaves clouds will replace her
Tears like a river
I need her like how a singer needs his voice
Like a priceless work of art that has lost its color
Something's gotta give if she's
missing from the picture
Love of my life
Predestined to be my wife
The one to grow old with
See our children's children
Trust me these aren't just feelings
These words are all true
For if I die with her in my sight
I know I'll wake to find beauty in my view
Beauty is not based solely on facial features
Some men only see a face

But that beauty fades to black
And never comes back
Beauty was when she loved me
When I was loved by no one else
Including myself
Locked within my shell she came to my rescue
Introduced me to the sun
Told me to throw away my tissue
And if I cry, try
To leave those tears on her shoulder
Now this shy guys is bolder
With my back towards my dark past
I can face our bright future
They say love leads to misery
Well in this crazy world
Loving her makes sense to me
I can die today with no care of tomorrow
I am the bow, beauty is my arrow
Wherever she goes my heart will follow
Bulls-eye, now we reunite
Beauty is placed back in her bow
Now we can watch our love grow
Through summer's heat
Through winter's cold
What is mine is hers
Whatever's hers is mine

If she's doing good I'm feeling fine
If she coughs
We're sick
But Vicks can't fix this
The cure does not reside in a bottle
Nor can it be contained by any seal
This love is real
That I feel for
Miss light skin
Miss dark skin
Miss short
Miss tall
With beauty standing by my side
I don't care about the fall

SHINE LIKE JESUS

Dark is the day
Dark is the night
Within this darkness there must be light
Light that oppresses the shadow of death
Light that conquers our darkest regret
Jesus is true light
All else is false
Jesus is pure light which regards not our faults

Come now Jesus and make bright these stairs I climb
Shine light Jesus on our doubts and fears
Don't let us fall lead us
For these stairs are hard and cold
Shine light Jesus so we'll know on what to hold

EARL

Earl McAbee you's a selfish man
You done upped and left me without a plan
The rent ain't been paid in God knows how long
Got Earl Junior out collecting cans
Two months from now the babies are due
And only God in heaven
Knows what the hell
You've been up to
The bill collectors stopped calling
They now make visits to the house
And I'm sitting here wondering what's next
Peeping through the window like I'm Malcolm X
Earl McAbee
You's a selfish man
You done died and left me with nothing in my hands
But you go on and Rest In Peace
While my heart lives in pieces

UNTITLED

Ignorance is very expensive
Yet and still poor people can't afford it
The price of living is so high
That the youth's forsake the mansion in the sky
And slay each other for the mansion in the hills
Abandoning their God given skills
Instead of helping to breathe the breath of life
We assist in taking
A husband from his wife
A father from his child
A son from his mother
Now there's another
Black woman kissing her baby goodbye

READ ALL ABOUT IT

Picked up the papers
To read bad news
War
Violence
Crime
We're living in perilous times
Crocodile tears from those who claim they care

For our common interest
But their claim to fame is vengeance.

HINDS

My tears become as a river
And the only thing left for me to do was give up
My rights
My life
And my sanity
Then the Lord smiled upon me
And said that I am beautiful
Made in his image
And molded by his hands
And that river
Which my tears had created
He did baptize me within

BETTY

What can this retched pen
Write of my aunty who is no more
Gone too soon
By the light of the moon
What can I write to comfort grandma
Through her many sleepless nights

CLOSET

There's a big closet in a dark room
In which all bad memories go
Some clinging to the ceiling
While others lie on the floor
Rekindled memories can never be forgotten
So be careful not to open this door
When placing
Your bad memory in
Slip it under along with your sins
Go back good memory
Do not enter that door
You belong in that small closet
With its small door

DISCONTENT

There was no reply to my cry
My burdens persist
While heartaches my heart won't resist
There was no water for the fire
That burnt my desire to see better days
There was no light
To brighten my dark path

So I stumbled then fell
Not wanting to rise again
There was no balm
For wounds unhealed
My storms had no calm
My fate then was sealed
There was no needle or thread
For my torn heart
So my heart remained rent
As I became discontent

ADDICT

Don't do drugs
Don't do life
For both lead to death
Better yet
Do sorrow
Do pain
So many are addicted to life
They never want to die
She's addicted to grief
Always want to cry
For she's not dying fast enough
The pain is too much

Aid is scarce

Billows are fierce

Arrows constantly pierce her already shattered heart

She wishes she could go back to the start

And take the other road

The one her mother pointed to

For she has been down both

She knows its hills

She knows that the street lights stay off

Even after the sun goes away

Still her daughter strays

As her mother's warnings fly through the other ear

Now its too late says fate

You're in too deep

And there's no route that leads you out

Some are addicted to drugs

Others are addicted to life

As for me

I'm addicted to disappointment

In love with misery

For they're the only one who has never abandoned me

MR WINDOW MAN

Keep on keeping on mister window man

Though the drugs have damaged your brain
The liquor has damaged your liver
You still have strong hands
Clean those windows
And those glass doors
So that men wearing suits and
ties can enter those doors
To sit in their corporate offices
Maybe one day they will pity you and leave a tip
But I'll leave advice
Keep on keeping on Mister window man
Though the drugs have weakened your back
You still have strong hands
To purchase your crack

HOME ALONE

Mother is on the phone
Praying with a church sister
Baby sister is on the floor combing her dolly's hair
Other sister writing in her diary "I wish I wasn't here"
Father is in his room
Screaming at athletes with deaf ears
I'm writing in a book
The things I see and hear.

MIX

A Jewish boy
With Palestinian skin
Cried with Arab eyes
For his mother lived on the other side
A Jewish God with Jewish eyes
Cried for the Jews the Palestinian killed
An Arab god with an Arab tongue
Pledged revenge the Arab blood we will
A Christian boy with Christian eyes
Cried with ink on paper for the
wrongs that are being done
To the children of the stone
And the children of the gun

ROBOTS

My mind is telling me to flee
Get away
Get away
For that brighter day I've looking for
Has gotten
Far away
The sun's rays don't shine no more my way

Oh lord I pray today

Make a way

Make a way

My heart is telling me this shouldn't be

I've got to

Make away

Make away

Out of this calamity

Oh Lord

Let it be

Let it be

The sun's rays are gonna shine on me someday

Today

And tomorrow

Freedom will follow

Robots we are robots

Just doing what THEY tell us

Buying the lies that THEY sell us

Once a child

Now I'm a grown-up

But I still don't know why

THEY laugh as we cry

We die

We die

THEY don't cry

Wont cry
We suffer it's a struggle to survive
Oh why don't THEY open THEIR eyes
Oh why can't THEY realize
No tissue for our tears
THEY don't care
THEY have no tissue for our tears
THEY don't care
Oh why
Oh why

POETS

Poets are lonely men and women
Who write of love
But of them love has never written
Tis easier to turn back the hands of time
Than to read poets mind
To know the pain written within each line
And to tell if they're fiction are true
Would surely make you a poet too

CHILD

Carry on child
Though me and your pa are gone
I know it's been a while child
But soon your weary head will get its rest
Your dishwashing hands will get a manicure
And your traveling feet a pedicure
Stay strong child
For the others are weak
Don't forget to visit
For tonight we left the memories at the creek
When times get hard child
Sing the songs we taught
Sing em when you buy the groceries tomorrow
Sing em when the kids search through
the things you bought
I see you've carried on child
And my promises did come true
You got a pedicure with new pretty white shoes
They gave your dishwashing hands a manicure
And white gloves
They put their pennies together
And bought you a pretty white dress
They made sure that you dressed to impress
And looked your best

In your pretty whit coffin

Where your weary head can now get its rest

IS ANYBODY THERE

Is anybody there

Does anybody care

Does anybody see what I see what I see

Poverty no charity

We are searching

We are seeking

For a good reason

To wake up in the morning

Mama I'm leaving, I'm leaving

Though I know I can't make it on my own

But father God will surely lead me home

This world is not my home I'm just traveling through

When I am gone friends I'll miss you

At times I am so scared

Because of what's out there

Corruption is all that I see

Tragedy

Negativity

They say that we can't make it

My joy they have replaced it

So day and night I'm weeping

Relieve me

Relieve me

WITHOUT GIVING REASONS

If paper could write back

It would speak of many words

Pens have left on his lines

Poems of chilling remorse with

heart-wrenching rhymes

Of roads straight and narrow

Crooked and wide

Filled with sorrow

And thoughts of suicide

If paper could write back it would change the tone

Of these somber thoughts

It would edit many words to give

them happy meanings

But pen would change them back

Without giving reason

FATHER TO SON

You've got to go to church boy
cause you's a church-boy
Go and find dem shoes you hid beneath the bed
And while you're at it go get your black pants
I saw in your closet
I bought you a shirt and tie
Go and try them on
I know you'll be looking mighty fine
I really don't know why you hate going to church boy
When you've been going your whole life
Well sure there's many grief and strife
But don't you know the day don't
come before the night
You've got to face the dark times
While searching for the light
I know I sound like a hypocrite son
For some things I tell you not to do I've already done
Yes I was a church-boy once
But those days have gone down along with the sun
I used to sing all those songs of praise
I used to sing hymns
Back then it was just Jesus and me
But when I became a man
I let go of Jesus' hand

Here's my tithes and offering son
Yours is on the table
I know you want me to come this week
But I'm not able
Don't forget to pray for me
But pray for yourself first
Before the evil days come nigh
And your better days become your worst
So go to church boy
Cause your mother grew you up in the church boy
I just want you to understand
That I want you to be what I never became
And that's a church-man

REFLECTION

The only way to view one's self
is to stare into a mirror
To see what you've become
You already know what you've turned into
But to view the change is monumental
Your eyes no longer glimmer with hope
Your lips are dry
Your skin now pale wonder if
you've forgotten of the sun

I live in a world of no reflection
Not even a shadow on the ground
I cannot see the monster that I've become
I've forgotten who I use to be
There exist no pictures to rekindle memories
Of a time when I smiled
A time long ago ancient and extinct
Mama told a story of when she saw
her reflection for the first time
She had me in her stomach headed to a river
Never to come back
To drown away her misery and a child not meant to be
But in the water she saw a woman with child
Staring back at her with tears in her eyes
So she stepped out that river never to return
Now I'm headed down to that same river
To finish what she was too scared to do
Oh suicide
I cannot hide
Ima hold on to pastor's hand and pray he don't let go
Get baptized in that same river
And killed this monster that I have become

HUMAN WARNING

Don't wait for someone to say those three words
You can first love them
In order to be helped you must first extend your hand
To be a good father
You must first become a better man
To overcome you must first understand
Cherish all that is
Refrain from judging your neighbor
The earth is getting warmer
As mans heart grows cold
This has happened before that
story has already been told
When we think to do good evil is present
And these things have been so since my adolescence
Search for a change
It can be found
Within the deepest of oceans
Or buried underground
If needs be change the way you live
Do not always accept but give
Love those who hate you
By doing so that person's love for you will grow
But do know as the song Bob sung goes
Friends will be enemies

And enemies friends

So then

Be wiser than the serpent

But harmless as a dove

Human warming is what I'm speaking of

I'm not black

Not white

Not dark

Not light

Not yellow

Or red

Not a negro

Not Caucasian

Not Filipino

Not Haitian

Not Jamaican

I am not from Barbados

Don't judge me from the size of my nose

The color of my eyes

Look beyond my accent and ancestry

Just see me

For I am not Cuban

But human

I am what you see when you look in the mirror

I am you

A citizen of planet Earth

WRITER'S BLOCK

I ain't got the blues
And I ain't got no other color
I've ran out of things to write about
I've already written words of my
mother, father, and sisters
I've written of God and Jesus
And Satan who rarely leaves my pen
I've also written of my many sins
I've written of tears
Which refuse to leave my eyes alone
I've written of life but mostly death
I've written of depression and its deeper depths
Which causes me to weep
But even Jesus wept
I've written of joy
But joy has no recollection of me
I've written of the moon and it's light
I've written of the stars which seems so close
But are yet so far
I've written of the un-fought fight
And lonely days which proceeded many lonely nights

WHO

Who has suffered more the Jew or the negro
Who would've benefited if had they
Not walked through life's door
If they had remained unborn
Not knowing the outside of their mother's womb
Whom
The rabbi says the Jews
The pastor says the slaves
Though I am the Pastor's son I cannot choose
They say the Jews betrayed Jesus
And the Negro's crime was being born black
So the oppressors considered that
And appointed a bullet to the Jew's head
And a whip for the Negro's back
Who did God cry for more
Were more tears shed for one than the other
After all a Jew called him father
Run Negro run Jew
Before the oppressors come
With their whips and guns

ONE MORE TIME

Life stared in the mirror and saw Death
Death said to Life
Aren't you ready yet
No said Life
I got more tears I gotta cry
And plus my heart has an appointment at nine
To get broken one more time

LOVE

Love; the most overused word in the English language
Yet the hardest to define
Is it because most people that use
the word are actually lying
Well since he's deceased
I guess I can't ask Saint Valentine

CURSED

I feel that I am cursed
For instead of getting better
Life gradually gets worse

Days seem longer
As my heart forgets to take its beats
My palms are always wet
And fear seems to be my only companion
This fright of the outside world
Keeps me locked within a box
With no door to let others in
And no window to stare at their backs

MAMA'S SKIRT

Don't forget to remember me
Though I've cost so much of your pain
And of your misery
I've known your cares
I know your cries
For I see my tears in your eyes
I've known your pain
I've felt your hurt
I see your tears on MAMA'S SKIRT
Where once laid mine
But soon you'll find
that at times
The only shoulders to lean are your own
Surrounded by all yet all alone

For eighteen years I've loved that smile
Formed only by your lips
Expressed only through your eyes
Eyes that not even tears are worthy to inhabit
So use our fondest memories
To blanket these new worries
No more bedtime stories
Those days are gone and done
But may our smiles be your pillow
When nightmares come
When your back and front
Lie against bricks called life
I'll be at both sides with outstretched arms
For I know your cares
I know your cries
For I've seen my tears in your eyes
I've known your pain
I've felt your hurt
I see your tears on MAMA'S SKIRT

THE BEACH IN CONNECTICUT

I miss the beach
The one time I remember us going
Is the only time I remember playing with my dad

We played a silly game
Where the object was to toss around a ball
And make sure it doesn't fall
I do not recall who won
Neither does my memories
Tell of the two other players
Not even the color of the ball
But I do know that the ball did in fact fall
And since that day he has hated me
And I have mirrored that same feeling back
Maybe someday we'll go back to that-
BEACH IN CONNECTICUT
Search for that happy-ball
And play that silly game.

BORROWED WINGS

There is no refuge here
As there is in the air
So give back my wings they are not yours
They belong not to creeping things
Wings are for birds
Without them I cannot fly
And being grounded I fear my demise
Like the only boat yet to leave the dock

I am the wingless bird without a flock
Give back what you have taken for
your feathered flights-
Are flown on borrowed wings
Your journeys are not genuine
Give back my wings I must ascend
Do it quickly
For your dreams are nearing its end

ENVY

I've never had to tell good days goodbye
Cause all I've ever seen was bad days go by
I've never had a home to call my own
All I've ever had was a broken home
I've never sung the star spangled banner
For in this land of the free
Freedom has never resided in me
I've never had the chance to wipe tears from my eyes
For I've never stopped crying
I've never had the chance to say I love you
For I have no one to say those words to
I've never
But I remember
That you always did

MEMORIES

Memories are for those who often forget
And not for those who often regret
My memories often fail to remind me of good times
And when happy am I
Bad memories come to spy
A place where only good memories reside
To remind good people of happier times
Do I often dream of
But that place had never been seen
Nor heard of in my past
And I doubt its existence in my future

BROKEN

You'd never know how black you are
Until you stand next to a white man
And you'd never know how rich you are
Until you give to a man who has nothing
A man who considers the ground to be his floor
And the sky to be his roof
He has no window to stare through
When it rains it pours on him
Even when there is not a cloud in sight
We speak of us having spirits broken

And hearts contrite
Yet we are blessed
For as Wyclef Jean said:
He knows some people so poor
When it rains is when they shower
If we consider ourselves broken then they're powder

SIGNS

People are sighing
Hopelessly the poor are dying
Mothers are crying for their sons
have not returned from war
And I see the falling stars
And I'd change it if I could
The moon has turned to blood
And the stains are on the ground
That's how I know your coming is sure
I see the signs of the coming of the Lord
Living in these times and we so
oft wonder where you are
But you are close even at the door
Much closer than before
Yes I know
Your coming is sure

Lord knows I'm trying

But these tears won't cease from falling

The youths are dying Lord

Not knowing just who you are

And I see the falling stars

And I'd change it if I could

The sun it shines no more

That's how I know your coming is sure

I know you're closer Lord

Than when I first believed

Satan is trying me

But your child he can't deceive

Yes I know your coming is sure

CANDLE

At times I feel like a candle in the sun

No benefit will come from my existence

And when night falls and the candle's light is out

There's never a match to be found

UMBRELLA

On a rainy day I saw a man with holes in his umbrella
So I pointed him out to another
Just take a look at that fella
Which one
The one with holes in his umbrella
It seems he just can't get it yet
Cause every rainy day he just keeps getting wet
Watch him
Walking around town
Head in the clouds
Feet on the ground
Smiling back at those who smile at him
But his heart would only frown
Telling jokes to those who love to laugh
But who don't even know the half
Now that's a sorry soul
If only his story were to be told
Or maybe written
But who would listen?
See here fella
It seems you're in a dilemma
How so
Well you got holes in your umbrella
The rain is seeping through
And it sure is soaking you
This old umbrella ain't helping you much
Thanks for your concern but I'm in a rush
Where you headed to
To church to pray my sins away

EARTH ANGEL (Dedicated to Althea Henry-Gordon)

Mama said that they'd be days like these
And mama you was right
But I've got to disagree with you
When you say there's no such
thing as love at first sight
For an angel has looked my way
More beautiful than a summer's day
Smile like ivory
Can't believe that she's in love with me
Tell me have you seen her
Who
My earth angel
Loving her feels so right
Love and lust have met in battle
And love has won the fight
To cherish her is my duty
Like Taurus said
She's a natural beauty don't need
no makeup to be a cutie
She's a queen
So surreal to be seen with her
My earth angel
Just the thought of Althea
Got me messing up my rhyme scheme

Where was I

Gotta concentrate

Try not to emulate those guys from her past

Promising that their love would last

Now they're M.I.A

Reluctant to A.S.K for her hand

So I stepped in

Now next to her I stand

My earth angel

She has a smile that can illuminate

the darkness in my soul

The one before left my heart in fractions

I know that she could make me whole again

Not only a friend but my empress

Former princess

All joy that comes with loving her I will possess

My earth angel

From her features and the scent of her perfume

You might assume

That my love for her was only merely infatuation

But that's not so in this situation

For others are beautiful but her beauty is rare

And I am like the panting deer

Which long not for water

But whose soul thirst for it does care

My earth angel

Her hair

Her lips

Her hands

Her eyes

To not love her makes me a fool

To do the opposite makes me wise

Yet wise men say "only fools rush in"

But I cannot hold back these strong feelings

Her love I'm needing

Like how the cactus needs the sun

Say my name and I'll come to your rescue

Can't picture myself not being next to her

All mine I will not share

Our love let no one put asunder

Love her even when we're both six feet underground

I have found the missing piece to my puzzle

Like Matisyahu

"there's only one woman for me other half of my soul"

In my heart it is summer

Though outside is cold

My earth angel

They say that lonely is the man without love

Well I'm not that man cause it's me she's thinking of

So what is a man without a woman

Is he not like a comb without honey

A fox without a hole

He is compared to a bird without a nest

Like sheep without a shepherd

Like leaves without a tree being driven by the wind

Carried away helplessly

Like a rainbow without colors

Like blind men who cannot dream

My earth angel

My dear this day I am complete

For I have found my rib, the other half of me

Flesh of my flesh, bone of my bone

I've got you so why would I roam to another heart

When today my life truly starts

My earth angel

She's the most beautiful thing

these eyes have ever seen

With a crown upon her head

And sweet kisses upon her lips

I am sure that she's heaven sent

My earth angel

Grow old with me my love

Our better days are yet to be

Yes I can see us together for a long time

Even after the sun and moon have lost its shine

And all the stars have fallen from heaven

I'll be the light for your day

And brighten your dark nights

Your battles I will fight
My earth angel
Earth angel
Earth angel
Will you be mine

BRAVERY

The tears of a mother are like no other
Especially the ones that are shed
for her child who is dead
Mama Africa is crying for her children
Former Africans who now claim to be American
Afro American of course
Victims who claim innocence
Victims of the system
Former slaves in present slavery
Slave where is your bravery
Is it etched in the bullet which took the life
Of the man who cried peace
Now he must rest in that peace
African where is your bravery
Is it carved in Jesus' nails
And the back of our ancestry
I wish not to die

Not to be crucified
But to live through the night
And behold the promised day
When Mama Africa
Finally has her peaceful sleep
And have her tears dried
By those who caused her to weep

FEBRUARY 28TH

Its funny how this came to me
On the last day of what they call
The month of black history
I remember Malcolm X saying
That growing up he was called nigga so often
He started thinking that it was his name
Well I know that nigga is not my name
For my birth certificate says otherwise
So why do I respond to nigga
Why do I get upset when a Hispanic
refers to me as such
Let's not blame the ones who created this word
Rather lets blame ourselves for proving them right
(we are ignorant)
If we continue this trend

Then we will lose our pioneers vision
Causing us to lose our sight and our dreams
Let's not wait until February to
look back on the struggle
Start today
Start now
I pen these words on February 28th

SLEEP WALKING

I'm in a nightmare with my eyes wide open
Trying to dream dreams in darkness
Searching for some light and still searching
Trying to figure out the meaning of life before dying
Asking them why but still complying
I'm still in this nightmare with my eyes wide open
Searching for a bed and still searching
Longing to rest my head
But still sleepwalking

HUNGER PAINS

He's homeless not hopeless
The house of God is a shelter not
ran by the government

That's where hope lives

She's got children with her

No food to fill her

Kids don't miss school cause that's

how they eat their dinner

Can't believe there is hungry people in America

That hurts me

No coats in December

That's worse B

They say time will tell but they got

hunger pains right now

Wow

Tried to stand but fell

Born in heaven raised in hell

Better off in a jail cell

Because at least you have somewhere to sleep

I weep and wish that things were better

But I'm starting with the man in the mirror

What can I do to help Mount Vernon,

Bronx, and Brooklyn

Where with guns and knives the youths are taken

Now mama sheds tears

Can't even pay for the funeral

So hard to even sleep

An intervention is crucial

SIGNATURE (Dedicated to Fitzroy and Olive Brown)

Life
Why have you given me divorce papers
Would you rather that I go to bed with death instead
Being caressed by Death's cold arms
And shivering though I am blanketed by its sheets
Now I sleep the sleep
For I have died the death
My years with you I do not regret
I have cherished each breath, even the last
You've been with me through all my ordeals
With you I've found the most beautiful OLIVE
Among the olive trees of the field
She has cried my tears
I have felt her pain
Her love lifted me when I was brought way down
By the cares of this earth
There has been many times wherein
I have refused to sign
Now I've come to realize
That the choice is no longer mine
There is a higher being who has intervened
He has handed me Death's pen
And demanded that I sign
So I write Fitzroy Brown

On the divorce paper's line

SHINE LIGHT JESUS

Dark nights and cloudy days got me missing the sun
Wondering why it has gone away
And when again will it come
Please shine light Jesus
On these broken stairs I climb
Then memories of the sun
Bid me be patient one more time
So I embrace my valley while waiting for better days

TWO DEATHS

One life to live
Two deaths to die
Love kills you first
Then a bullet closes your eyes
Forever distracting them from the prize
That lies beyond the skies
But does there exist a heavenly home
For this earthly sinner
Who was born in sin

And dies therein
Your beginning is smooth
Yet your end is rough
But God knows best
So he grants sweet rest
To those who are tired of life
Who were dragged through dirt
Before being buried in it

FOUR SEASONS OF MAMA

When mama came home knocking
snow from her boots
That meant winter had arrived
When mama came home and exchanged
Flowers from her hair to mine
That meant it was spring time
When mama came home at nine
And the sun had still not lost its shine
That taught me of summer
When mama did not come home
They told tales of stairs
And a tragic fall
And that taught me of autumn

I AM BEAUTIFUL TOO

I am beautiful too
Look at these brown eyes
Take a look at these full lips
Now watch me smile
It's been a while but I'm proud to be an African child
(Love you Mama Africa)
You hate me yet you dress as I do
You hate me yet our tongues are the same
You hate me yet you bite my style
You even walk as I do
My brown skin shines even brighter in the sun
The same sun that has looked upon me
And has blessed me with its beams
I am redeemed by the blood of the lamb
Yet my blood is still being shed
Too many blacks are dead because
we don't love ourselves
Our hair is now straight
Our stars bleach their skin
Not realizing that they are still black within
I too sing
I also dance
I cry
But those tears go unnoticed

BLOOD

My own is against me
So should I seek foes for refuge
My blood is refused by their veins
Let it rain
Let it rain
Pluck the strings of the violin
For their lies emptiness within
The ring of sorrow is whole
While the ring of joy is broken

CHEEKS

Mama's tears are on both sides
But sometimes she cries with no
tears coming from her eyes
The pain she felt never affected the love she gave
And in her life pain is all she gained
Mama's tears are like no others
They're bigger than mine
Yet smaller than her mothers
The tear's long streaks
Stayed on mama's
Black and blue cheeks

To remind us that what she went
through was no small feit
But there were rear occasions
when a smile would appear
On mama's tattered face
And that usually meant
She was in a state of grace
Now papa's tears are on both times
Cause the last time he struck mama
Was the last time she cried.

CRADLE OR GRAVE

Life after life is my humble plea
For this life without death brings nothing but agony
A save haven from these struggles yet I will seek
Please pardon me from this table of sorrow
But save a seat at the table of joy
From the cradle to the grave
Is a sad reminder
Of lives God took after he gave
But in the end I'll choose the cradle
And curse the grave

SHOE BOX POETRY

I hug the shoe box which holds my poetry
And shed tears upon the bits of papers
I do not know why I write
But still I write
I'm confused for these words
Which come from my troubled heart
Seem to comfort and encourage others
But for some strange reason
They do not comfort me

MY ANGEL

(In loving memory of Sis Campbell)
They say it's too cold outside for angels to fly
well I mourn this day for my angel has died
so I tried borrowing her wings
knowing they are not my own
wrapped them around me hoping
you would come home.

The love I have for you is like a lion to his cub
oh I miss her love
but destiny is like the tears I shed for you this day

but I won't cry too long cause I'll meet
you by the river someday.
the same one where Jesus walked on its water
Sitting in the second pew of the church
rocking to the music singing to the melody
and writing notes in her pad
these are the fondest memories we had

It is often said: don't cry it was meant to be
so why can't these tears stay away from me
her soul has gone back to her maker
so we're looking at old pictures laughing and crying
but the tears surpassed the laughter

Black suits and ties
black hats tilted to show the other side.
It was her time her number was on the clock
her day was on the calendar
Whether umbrellas or fans
tears with napkins in hand
trying to hold back the tears
but got sunglasses just in case

She's in a better place
ashes and dust
are replaced by streets of gold

for now we can only speak in our dreams
So I spend my days longing for the night

You will truly be missed
but I know you're in Glory rocking to the music
and singing to the melody.

They say it's too cold outside for angels to fly
well I mourn this day for my angel has died.

ABOUT THE AUTHOR

Lenford Mawell Thompson was born in the island of Jamaica on May 17, 1985 to Linford Thompson and Faith Brown. His years of childhood in the small village of Joe Hut, Trelawny were pleasant surrounded by his large extended family and his younger sister Kadesja Thompson. He attended FreemansHall Primary School and at the age of 9, Lenford, Kadesja and their parents migrated to the United States.

His first days in America could be described in two words; culture shock. He was lost, everything seem congested and everyone spoke a sort of English he had never heard before. However as time progressed, Lenford adapted to his surroundings and eventually was Americanized.

His love for poetry and writing ironically was found in Summer School after failing his 11th grade English class. His Summer School teacher introduced him to his favorite poet, Langston Hughes, and he immediately fell in love with his art form. Lenford then began writing stories, poetry, and sharing with friends, family and his church congregation. They all loved his work and would always ask for more. One of Lenford's dearest friends that he looks up to as an older sister, Carleen Richards, suggested that he turned his poetry into music. Thus discovering another passion of Lenford's and a deeper creativity from within. His music has touched many hearts and at times have brought people to tears.

At the age of 17, Lenford was diagnosed with depression and taking anti-depressants to get through each day. Though his depression still remains as an everyday struggle, in everything he does he leans on God. His faith has brought him to where he is today as well as his family. Lenford decided to write this book to share his story and inspire someone with his words.

Printed in the United States
By Bookmasters